colour inspiration
creative schemes to transform your home

conran
OCTOPUS

First published in 2002 under the title *100% Kleur*
by Sanoma Uitgevers B.V.
Capellalaan 65, 2132 JL Hoofddorp
Netherlands
© VT Wonen, Sanoma Uitgevers B.V. Hoofddorp 2002

This edition published in 2003 by Conran Octopus Limited
a part of Octopus Publishing Group
2–4 Heron Quays, London E14 4JP
www.conran-octopus.co.uk

Editor-in-Chief Makkie Mulder

Art directors Janine Couperus, Elise Yüksel

Image coordination and composition Heleen van Gent

Line-extension coordinator Mieke Beljaarts

Project editor Linda Pijper

Text and final editing Juliette Berkhout

Styling coordinator Nina Monfils

Photography
Alexander van Berge, Dennis Brandsma, Hotze Eisma, Paul Grootes, Luuk Geertsen, René Gonkel, Jip van Hengst, Ewout Huibers, Peter Kooijman, Anneke de Leeuw, Eric van Lokven, Otto Polman, Femke Reyerman, Joyce Vloet, Hans Zeegers

Styling
Julia Bird, Frans Bramlage, Fietje Bruijn, Nans van Dam, Marjan Godrie, Kristel de Jong, Jet Krings, Linda Loenen, Marianne Luning, Evelien Nuyten, Mirjam Roskamp, Jacqueline Roeleveld, Mirella Sahetapy, Reini Smit, Caroline Tilgenkamp, Frans Uyterlinde, Petra de Valk, Nicolette de Waard, Valerie van der Werff

Illustrations Heleen van Gent

With thanks to:
Daniëlle Aarts, Flamant Home Interiors, Sandra Groenendal, Johan Heino, Bob Jansen, Willeke Jongejan, Liliana Kootstra, Dirk van der Meer, Yvonne Mulder, Babs Pierik, Laila Skipper Rasmussen, Nathalie Steenmeijer, Manon Suykerbuyk, Hans Ultee, Madelon Vink, Hans Vrijmoed

Publisher Peter Schönhuth

Printing coordination Mieke Dekker

Lithography Litho Spirit

Printed by Valprint

UK edition translated by First Edition Translations Limited

Jacket design Carl Hodson
Additional text and editing Ali Hanan

British Library Cataloguing-in-Publication Data. A catalogue record for this book is available from the British Library.

ISBN 1 84091 328 2

4

'Mere colour, unspoiled by meaning,
and unallied with definite form, can speak
to the soul in a thousand different ways.'

Oscar Wilde

contents 7

Colours make the world beautiful and exciting, they attract or repel, alert us or make things recognizable. Colours have long been a source of fascination for people. We have always had the urge to colour things and we are preoccupied, almost obsessively, with the colours of our clothes and homes. Paint is the most effective, versatile, fool-proof and budget-friendly decorating material in which to experiment with colour. Every age, every culture has celebrated paint, and when you brush it on to your furniture or walls, you pay homage to a time-honoured tradition. Whether adorning a body in ritual, coating lips or decorating a whole town, like Jodhpur, swathed in the Hindu Brahmin caste's royal blue, paint is part of life's colour. From creating mood antidotes to reshaping a home's architecture, paint and colour have the power to transform the way you live – and all in a brushstroke.

In centuries gone by, colour was a labour of love. Our ancestors ground lapis lazuli, crushed ochre, smashed beetles, and brushed toxic white lead on to their walls in pursuit of colour. Now, in the twenty-first century, we live in an era of readymade, available paints. There are thousands of colours to choose from, but most of them are just languishing in the dust of DIY stores. Strangely we are afraid of splashing out in colour. In the United Kingdom, the chart topper of the best-selling interior paints is oh-so-safe magnolia, while the most radical of the top ten is indigo. Sixties design maverick Verner Panton, whose funky, psychedelic colour schemes now define the era, declared there should be a tax on white, the most neutral of all paints. His life's work was dedicated to 'provoking people into using their imaginations.'

'Most people spend their lives in dreary grey-beige conformity, mortally afraid of using colour... I try to show new ways to encourage people to use their fantasy and make their surroundings more exciting.' *Verner Panton*

Colour – as Johannes Itten, who taught colour theory at the Bauhaus school in Germany in the Twenties, showed – is deeply personal and intensely subjective. He explored the concept of personal aura, the idea that everyone has a set of individual colours. In 1928 Itten gave his students various combinations to paint with. After half an hour he discovered some of the mixes were making them edgy and irritated. He then asked them to try painting with a combination that they found personally harmonious. Itten discovered the palette they preferred was mirrored in their own colour choices, right down to the clothes they were wearing.

Most of the way we choose colour is purely instinctive. Yet we understand something of the colour spectrum. Aristotle for example, believed blue and yellow were the true primary

living with colour

colours, reflecting the earth's dictators of light, the sun and moon. Yellow, he thought, was the first colour to come out of the light and blue the last to return to the darkness. All other colours came in between as the sun made its long journey throughout the day.

Colour is, in fact, intangible, as Sir Isaac Newton discovered at the beginning of the eighteenth century. Colour is no more than a reflection of light on a surface; without light there is no colour. When Newton shone white light through a triangular prism, he discovered the light coming from the prism splintered into seven different colours, each with their different wavelengths. By understanding the wavelengths of colour we understand how we perceive it. Beauty as Newton showed, really is in the eye of the beholder. As light strikes an object, the object absorbs all the light, except the wavelength it reflects back at us. As white is a result of all colours mixed into one, it reflects all wavelengths, which is why an empty space painted white looks so spacious. In contrast, black absorbs almost every wavelength: it is a 'black hole', and in design black retreats and looks more enclosed.

The brain responds to different wavelengths: the eye has to make the most adjustment for red (which has the longest wavelength), but hardly any for blue (which has the shortest wavelength). Imagine a red traffic light, which shouts 'stop' compared to a restful green for 'go'. The colour of an object is the first thing the brain registers about it, which is why it's so critical to design. It shapes our first impressions and reactions to a design.

'Without colour there is no form.'   *Johannes Itten*

Colour's wavelengths resonate within us. Red raises the metabolic rate by thirteen per cent and makes our hearts beat faster, while green calms us, slowing down our breath. When light strikes the iris it's converted to electrical impulses travelling to the hypothalamus, the part of the brain presiding over our hormones and endocrine system. In microseconds, a physiological reaction takes place and, in time, so does a psychological response, depending on our previous experience of a colour. Some of this is very personal, as Itten's students revealed. You may love the silvery blue sheen of a wall for the simple reason that it reminds you of your mother's aquamarine ring. For you, this hue brings comfort and love. For someone else this blue may be austere and aloof. Colour is defined by the mind's eye.

'When I choose a colour it is not because of any scientific theory. It comes from observation, from feeling, from the innermost nature of the experience in question.'   *Henri Matisse*

11

The odd thing is we don't even have the language to describe what we see. A study into language in the Sixties by the anthropological duo Berlin and Kay discovered many cultures only had two basic words, 'light' and 'dark'. Out of the 98 languages studied, English had the widest word palette, with eleven words: black, white, red, orange, yellow, green, blue, pink, grey, brown and purple. For all the other colours, words are adopted from visual references, like aubergine, avocado, rose and turquoise. References elaborate on the few words we have, like 'pea green', 'sky blue' or 'hot pink'. So there it is. Colour defies description. And, considering computer graphics have now created no less than sixteen million different nuances of colour, it's a linguistic relief.

'I found I could say things with colour and shapes that I couldn't say any other way – things I had no words for.'   *Georgia O'Keeffe, artist*

Yet while colour defies description, we often use colour to describe the way we feel. We 'see red', go 'green with envy' and 'get the blues'. 'Colour', as Carl Jung once said, 'is the mother tongue of the subconscious.' Colour ignites our moods and emotions.

On a practical level we can also harness its powers of illusion by using the qualities of a colour's light-absorbing or reflective properties. Colour can be used to create a sense of space or fashion a cosy den. A single colour can make a room seem cold or hot, spacious or small, inviting or formal. Nothing personalizes an environment or provokes a response like colour. It gives you the opportunity to make a personal statement, to stamp your interior with your unique personality and to create a place where you can feel at home. The joy of introducing colour through the use of paint is that it is so easy and inexpensive to experiment. You can repaint your home – or just a single wall – whenever you feel inspired.

With this book you can discover a world full of colour through paint. Divided into chapters dedicated to different hues, including white, blue, green, red, multicolour, black-grey-white, naturals, pastels and gloss and glitter, it examines each one, its folklore, its history and how it makes us feel. The final chapter, 'Colour in practice', gives you down-to-earth advice on how to choose paint and how to apply it, right down to the details. This chapter helps you to think about which colours are right for you and includes all the 'rules' of combining colours, then tells you how to break them. By the end of this book you will know what to consider when choosing the set of hues that makes you feel truly at home.

white

pearl   powder   blossom   cream   down

cloud   magnolia   milk

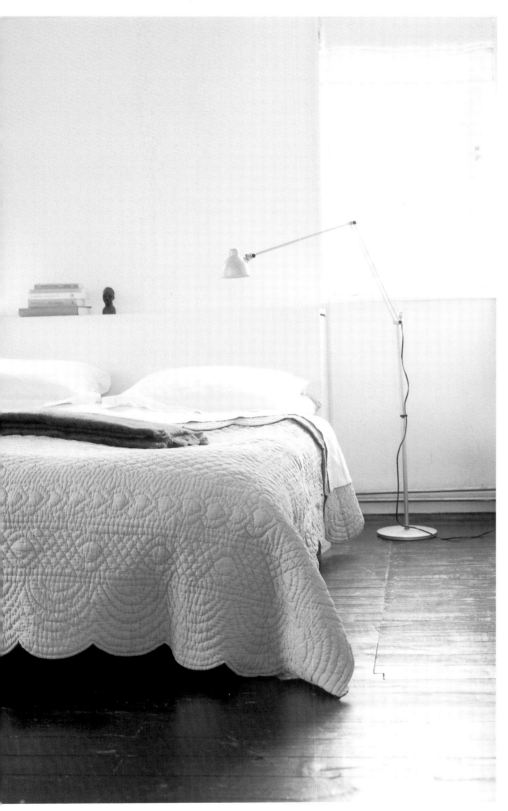

Within white lives so many different shades, such as the cool milky white in the bedroom (above), the warmer cream used for the modern hallway (opposite, left) and shades of powder white and rosy white on the woodwork in the hall (opposite, top right). White emphasizes textures, like the interplay of light and shadow on the baroque chair (above, right).

17

White is a tonic. White is the colour of peace and innocence, of calm and comfort, of simplicity and romance. It radiates freshness, clarity, purity and beauty and so is gratifying, timeless, fresh and bright. Walk in from a whirlwind day and a white interior is the calm eye of the urban storm. Its tranquil tones soothe and calm. Artists have used white as a canvas for centuries. And, in interiors, white makes the perfect backdrop for living. As interior *doyenne* André Putman once remarked: 'Life comes with its own colour: your friends, flowers, things. So you don't need much colour in your own interior.' In white surroundings, your beautiful possessions take centre stage. If they, too, are white, the emphasis falls on the subtle dance between light and shadow. Textures come to life: the fine weave of a white linen curtain, the sculptural relief of a white marble fireplace. White is the purist of colours, reflecting all light. Oddly, pure white is not a single colour at all but all colours whirled together to create white light. Yet white is hardly ever seen in its purist form. Even 'brilliant white', one of the most popular whites, is actually quite blue. As minimalist architect John Pawson once said: 'there are more than fifty shades of white'. From the soft cream of eggshells to the vibrant shades of magnolia, white has many moods. It is a chameleon, adapting to any interior. A minimal interior demands brilliant white while creamy whites are beautiful in more traditional interiors. Cream, white's more refined cousin, is soft and warm and combines beautifully with natural colours. Brilliant white is dazzling and fresh, lending strength to other colours. In any space, white reflects and radiates. And decorators know this. When choosing how to decorate a room, many designers begin with an entire whitewash. To select a palette, they watch the artful interplay of light on its journey around the room throughout the dawn, day, twilight and night. For white is tinted with pink at dawn, yellow in the day and blue at night. Once the designer gets a feeling for the light, colour is introduced, added bit by bit. White allows each colour to have its own presence. Once it was a lowly, utilitarian colour used as a limewash for the exterior of peasant's homes. With the advent of titanium white in the Twenties, it became accessible, first championed as fashionable by society decorator Syrie Maugham. Her *de rigeur* London living room featured white satin sofas, white Louis XV chairs, white velvet lampshades and a riot of flowers in various shades of plaster, oyster and Chinese white. Overnight, white-on-white became a classic, which blew over in a snowstorm to the interiors of Hollywood's rich and famous. White is simply a colour that complements all colours and is the colour for all seasons. White lets a house breathe. It cools down a home in warm climes, like the breezy whites of Moroccan interiors. And, it brings light to cold climates, like those in Scandinavia. So start with white, the backdrop for life.

The floor has been painted in milky white and then given a coat of floor varnish.

'Light, for me, is of paramount importance when I design a space. White space provides a perfect context for the play of **light** and **shadow**. Space, if it is perfect, does not require constant updating or redesigning. For me the changing quality of the light within a room according to the time of day and the season is enough.'

John Pawson, architect

Do as interior designer Syrie Maugham once did and create an all-white room. The array of whites here highlight the various textures with light and shadow, from the smooth lines of the table and the soft cushions to the rough shag of the floor rug and fine weave of the sofa throw.

23

24 In this bright, light house, where rooms merge into one another and continually offer glimpses into other rooms, all of the walls and ceilings have been painted in pale cream. When you walk from room to room, this scheme gives the whole house a sense of unity. These soft colours marry well with natural materials, such as the wooden floor, skirting boards and benches.

The white theme doesn't stop there. To keep the entire space airy and light, accessories such as the sofa, table top and side table are all white. However, to create a counterpoint, the skirting boards are in the same wood as the floor, making the floor space look larger. This home illustrates how white gives an illusion of spaciousness, perfect for small spaces.

25

1 powder 2 blossom 3 down 4 wool 5 milk 6 chalk
7 pearl 8 cream 9 quartz

White is the foundation for all colour and style combinations. In the first place, white-on-white is simple and yet sophisticated, as illustrated in the bedroom opposite. Only one shade of white has been used here – a milky white, giving the bedroom a peaceful, spacious, radiant light. Everything has been given a coat of creamy paint to create a gleaming effect. However, combinations with different textures such as a matt paint, chalky whitewash and a wide variety of materials (soft lambs' wool, coarse linen, shiny plastic, rugs) also work well with white, as they place highlights on rough and smooth textures. White is the foundation for countless colour combinations: it is fresh when used with bright colours, makes pastels less sugary, creates harmony with natural colours and is the only colour that softens black.

28

This kitchen makes the most of all the beautiful hues of white. The walls of this high-ceilinged, airy space have been painted in a milky white, the floor painted in the pale brown-grey of pearl (under a coat of floor varnish) and the row of cabinet doors below the curved skylight have been given a coat of a soft chalky white, a warmer white to prevent the interior from feeling

too clinical. To soften the sleek lines, the beech wood chairs bring in a feeling of natural warmth. The crockery on display in an open industrial-style aluminium shelving unit, rather like a gallery, reveals various sculptural shapes of a huge range of white objects, from soft rolls of kitchen tissue to curvaceous milk jugs. Simple objects look almost like a still-life in white.

29

White is so versatile. It is at home in any room of house. If it gets dirty, all you need to do is spring clean it with a new coat of paint. From living rooms to bedrooms, bathrooms to kitchens, a fresh layer of white is all it takes to make a room feel fresh, bright and clean. White is often at home in a kitchen or bathroom, perhaps because of its past associations with clinical spaces. One of white's previous incarnations has been as limewash, once used for hospitals and as a breathable sealing plaster for building exteriors. And, it's still used today. Whether you use limewash or another white, the pure lightness of white makes an interior feel hygienic, freshly scrubbed. In the bathroom, white feels sanitary – and calm. The bathroom is one of the few private spaces in the home where we can lock the door on the world and completely relax. And, white, a visual tonic, provides a neutral colour to allow us to unwind, physically and mentally. It feels clean and serene, plus it creates the optical illusion of space, perfect for small bathrooms. In the kitchen (opposite, left), white offers a neutral background for a culinary workshop. Use it as a backdrop to hang sculptural utensils and shiny pots and pans, (see opposite, right). Ultimately we like to eat from white plates because food simply looks so inviting on a white backdrop, like an edible form of art. In addition, a white tablecloth provides an endless variety of style options for dining: think of a traditional table setting in white-on-white with crystal and white porcelain or as a stunning backdrop for red and black glazed dishes from the Far East. A white bedroom is restful to the eye and the spirit. From crisp white linen sheets to a soft lambs' wool rug, a simple all-white bedroom creates a feeling of clarity and tranquillity, just the thing for sweet dreamy sleep. White needs to be used with care in a living room. Avoid too many cool tones as it needs to feel welcoming. A cold white can feel sterile and unfriendly. Choose warm-hearted whites instead, like magnolia, cream, pearl or rosy whites.

blue

night

twilight

dream

fresh

sea

water

mist

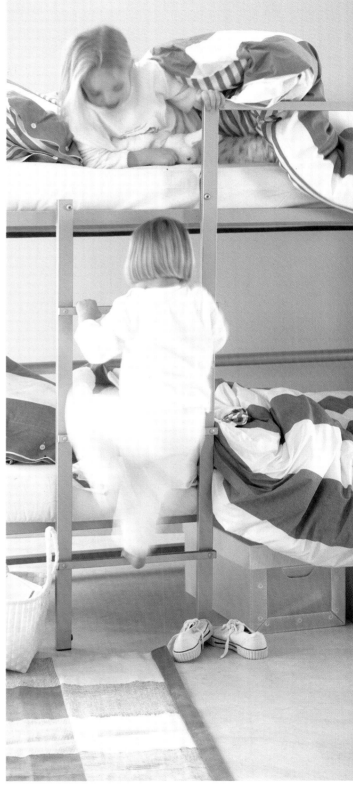

There's every reason to get the blues. A deep blue creates dramatic contrasts in a living room (opposite, centre). A fresh aqua blue is vivacious (opposite, below). And, a blue with overtures of purple has a sense of mystique (above, left). Another side of blue is gentle and subdued, like the quiet watery blue on the wall of the children's bedroom (above right).

35

Ask a crowd of people which is their favourite colour and more than half of them will say blue. But why is it so universally loved? Blue is soothing and fresh, the colour of the sky and the sea. It is infinite, full of possibility. It is the colour of two vital elements for living: air and water. Blue is timeless. For many centuries in Western art, blue was a sacred colour: ultramarine came from costly lapis lazuli and was reserved for the regal robes of the Madonna in the Middle Ages. And, because it was so expensive, blue was the preserve of the rich, hence 'royal blue'. Often used for royal courtiers, blue has become the colour of service, as worn by police officers, prisoners, traffic wardens and naval officers. Yet blue has inspired many modern painters: Picasso with his celebrated blue period, Yves Klein with his intense deep blue, Matisse with his characteristic blues from the south of France. Colour therapists believe blue is the colour of the intellect. Blue calms the pulse and inspires reflection. Strong blues stimulate clarity of thought and lighter softer blues still the mind and aid concentration. And, because blue quietens us, colour psychologists believe it helps communication. Within blue there are so many shades. Shades of blue inspired by the elements are always the most loved. Blue is cooling, peaceful and neutral. It soothes and calms. It has distance and depth. It is a many-sided colour, seen in shades of fresh aqua to cryptic purple, from gentle light blue to the deep blue of night. Aqua colours are fresh, minty, peaceful, and calming. In addition to these, there are the more neutral blues, such as comforting light blue and the timeless classics of denim and navy. Blue is a cool colour but also comes in warmer shades, particularly when it tends towards purple. Mix up fiery red and calm blue, of sky and earth to create purple, the colour of mysticism and magic. With white undertones of red, blue leans towards softer shades of purple, like lavender, mauve and indigo. Blue has many natural companions. Take blue and white, a fresh, light classic, dating from the seventeenth century when Chinese porcelain graced Western lives. Later, it was seen in the sky blue and white potteries of Wedgwood and Delft tiles. After centuries of use, it's no longer exotic, seen in everyday life in the ubiquitous look of blue jeans and white shirts, tiles, checked gingham fabrics and ticking. As blue and yellow live well together in nature, they also marry well in interiors. Different shades of blue and yellow combine equally well, like royal blue and gold, Prussian blue and egg-yolk yellow, sky blue and wheat gold. Try old and new combinations with blue.

The walls behind these shelves are painted in a misty blue.

'For more **intimate** rooms, choose shades of blue, which is the colour of **inner life**. Remember, the home is like a beautiful dress, tailored to the personality of the individual.'

Federico Sartor,
United Colors of Benetton

40

If blue is the colour for you, it's easy to paint your walls, floors or ceilings in this hue. Alternatively, to transport this expressive colour from home-to-home invest in blue furniture like the suite in this living room. These beautiful blues are enhanced by neutral, natural shades.

Light, greyish blue has a subtle effect and restful appeal. Once the colour of the Gustavian period of eighteenth-century Sweden, it is now a classic. When combined with grey and white, blue becomes warmer, more inviting. In the examples on this page, tones of grey-blue have been combined throughout the whole house with fresh whites and other soft natural

colours. The broad stripes on the wall behind the desk (opposite left) create a strong, graphic effect, yet when painted with gentle tones are not overpowering. The warm purple-blue used on the wall behind the armchair creates a soft contrast against the hard-edged concrete floor (centre). Behind the closet a watery blue colour creates a cool counterbalance (right).

43

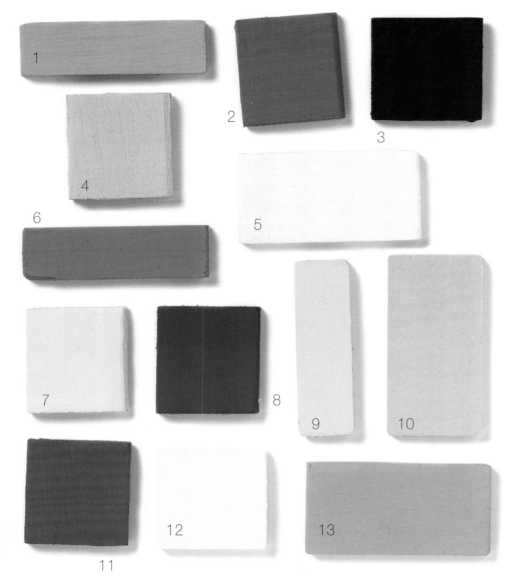

1 dream 2 sky 3 midnight 4 fresh 5 milk 6 spray
7 mist 8 indigo 9 water 10 sea 11 smoke 12 cream
13 twilight

Blue is not only peaceful. In its warmer incantations blue has a sense of humour, illustrated in this child's bedroom, where several different tones have been used. Here there's a strong dark bluish purple in the recess for the child's bed and floor rug, a softer shade on the other walls and a brisk white for the woodwork. In fact, blues always go well together, from pale, dusky blues to the stronger, greener blues and dark, anemone-coloured shades. Blue looks fresh combined with white, mysterious combined with purple, and stylish combined with green and grey. It's exceedingly bright, light and fun when complemented by orange or yellow. Light blue also works well with all types of brown, from light beige to chocolate, creating a timeless look. For a feeling of grandeur, add slivers of gold or silver.

45

Blue is reminiscent of air and water, two of life's essential elements. This age-old duo makes us feel peaceful and relaxed. Imagine how you feel with your toes dug in soft yellow sand, the sea stretching out in front of you in a mass of undulating blues till it meets the huge infinity of sky blue. The expanse of sand and sea and the fresh, clean salty air is a tonic to soul and body. So blue finds its home in rooms where you let yourself dream: bathrooms and bedrooms. Classic colours for the bathroom are the greener blues, such as aqua and turquoise, the fresh, energetic shades of blue that remind us of the ocean. However, other shades of blue also work surprisingly well in the bathroom, such as a soft, greyish blue that is both serene and restful, or a dark purple blue. Opposite shades apply to the bedroom, a place to let your thoughts waft in pale, cool blues. Blue and purple are the colours of twilight that invite us to think, feel, meditate and dream. Lavender is universally known for its mediative, healing properties, which makes it a perfect colour to sleep with. Rich purplish blues are dream-like, arcane, intimate and even a little magical. In the room opposite, you can see how aquamarine has an alert, energetic feel to it. Yet while bedrooms and bathrooms are the obvious places for blue, this hue is also at home in workspaces and living rooms. Studies have shown how in lighter shades, blue, particularly indigo, focuses the mind, so use it lavishly in your home office. As blue is also recognized as the colour of communication, it is suited to living rooms, where people meet and talk. Try a light blue, which makes a living room seem larger and calmer or grey-blue colours, which are subdued, atmospheric and create a sense of space. Pale blue is elegant and combines well with turquoise in a silvery interior. Use heavy blues with caution, as it is these shades which emphasize the cold, gloomy side of the colour, where rooms become blue with cold. Only use in conjunction with light, bright sunny colours, like spikes of hot orange, butter yellow or fiery reds.

green

| serenity | avocado | apricot flesh | star |

Bring nature's favourite colour indoors. Whether you paint one wall or use a few fresh accents, green injects vitality. A bright green dominates the wall behind the table (opposite). The shades used in the studio apartment are more subtle: green armchairs complement the stripes of colour on the wall (above). A green kitchen wall provides a lively canvas (below right).

51

Green is nature's favourite colour. It cloaks the earth, clothes tree trunks and branches and provides a pedestal for flower heads. For Mother Nature, in every season green is the new black. She changes her robe subtly, from the fresh, bright greens of new shoots in spring to the deep evergreen firs of winter. Because green is ever present, we intuit deep within our psyche that wherever there is green there is life. Green is our visual oasis. Seeing it relieves stress and gives us a sense of wellbeing, even in the fast-lane of urban life. Having green in view immediately improves the way we feel. A study of patients showed that those with a view on to a green garden had a quicker recovery time than those without. Green is healing. Its ability to restore energy and encourage growth is celebrated by the time-honoured oriental art of feng shui. History has demonstrated a variety of ways in which green has been distinctively used. The ancient Egyptians, renowned for copying nature into their interiors, used green on the floors of their temples. In the West, the Christian pastors wear green vestments at Easter, signifying rebirth and renewal. In colour therapy, green signifies balance, love and self-control. In every culture, green stands for stability, certainty and productivity. Green too, has been utilized by eco-conscious designers. After the oil crisis of the Seventies, the 'green' movement brought the hue indoors. The look was earthy, all olive green, chocolate browns and orange. Fresh leafy green reminds us of new life. And, it reminds us to respect it. We mark green's deep association with nature by the names that we give its colours: leaf green, forest green, apple green, lime green, mint green, pea green, olive green, moss green, copper, jade or emerald green. There are thousands of different greens, from pale grey-green to strong bottle green to the dark, brooding green of a pine forest. Add just a pinch of blue or yellow and green changes its character. Bluish greens, such as sea green, are cool and calming. As it edges towards yellow, green becomes livelier. Lime, for example, unifies the serenity of pure green with the vivacious energy of yellow. Yellow, according to colour therapists, is the colour of creativity and communication because it activates the brain and nervous system. Goethe, an expert on the subject of colour, had his study painted yellow. And, Van Gogh spent his life searching for the perfect yellow, as can be seen in the many vibrant shades in his famed sunflower paintings. Yellow, like the sun, radiates warmth. Anyone finding bluish greens too placid or subdued can instead, choose yellow-green or use blue in combination with yellow: a spirited, more vigorous and modern alternative. Bright yellow-green lime is a colour well suited to giving a cheerful flavour to a dark, neutral interior. Faded, greyish shades of greenish yellow evoke a more nostalgic mood. Follow the advice of feng shui and bring green into your interior. A shot of green brings equilibrium into our topsy-turvy lives.

53

On the walls is a quiet serene green.

'**Fresh**, **organic**, **elemental** – these are notions I associate with the colour green. It is a colour I use a great deal in my work, bright tonic greens in my summer collections, and more subtle greens in my winter collections. Green is not a colour, but an **entire palette**, with each shade evoking a different emotion, a different subconscious image.'

Ozwald Boateng, fashion designer

Yellow becomes quieter and less brilliant as it tends towards brownish green. This mustard
tone is certainly striking, yet also surprisingly classic. It feels fresh in combination with the
white and looks elegant set against the grey of the armchair. The dark colours of the curtains
and side table provide a sense of depth and contrast.

57

58

This house illustrates the vast tonal range of green. Here, in the living room (above left), nature has been invited in using a variety of tones. The dark, grey-green wall and the yellow-green furniture in the living room combine with the wood floor, mirror frame and the dark wicker chairs. Different shades of green glass (above, centre) in sculptural forms give the allure of a

traditional, chance still life. The sage-green painted cabinet (above right) against the wall near the dining table evokes the dormant evergreens of winter. Harmony prevails throughout due to the natural effect of greens in combination with other subtle shades of neutral colours. While the overall mood is serene, shots of green give this interior a quiet, restful energy.

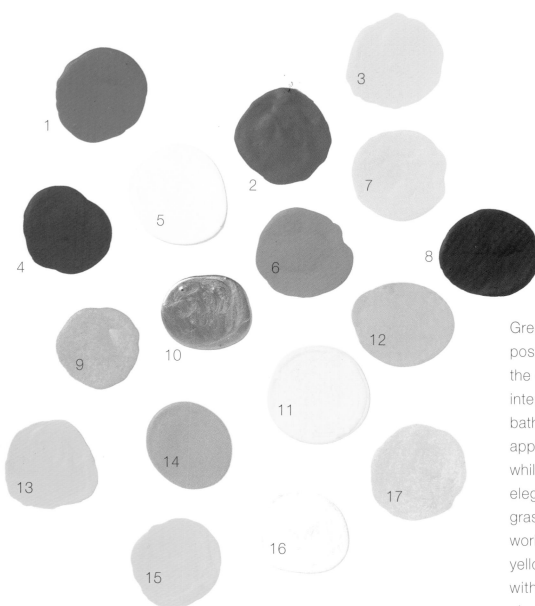

1 tarragon 2 sage 3 skin 4 spearmint 5 cream
6 mustard 7 celadon 8 fern 9 buttercup 10 sun
11 star 12 fresh 13 pinewood 14 serenity 15 peach
16 milk 17 pistachio

Green is restful. Yet at the same time, it possesses a natural energy, depending on the quantity and intensity of the greens in an interior. For example, sea green is at home in bathrooms. And, as an alternative to blue, apple green with white is fresh and timeless, while a dark green and creamy white looks elegant. A combination of turquoise with grass green and blue-green with linden green works well, as does grey-green with bright yellow. The darker combination of olive green with red, brown and gold is warm and glowing, and a room using only shades of yellow, lime and white sings of a spring-like optimism. Green harmonizes with natural materials, like earthenware, concrete, brick and wood, illustrated in the living room, opposite. It's no surprise that green always blends in with natural colours.

A yearning for nature resides in our bones. A view of green tells us stories of fields, glades and woods, of gardens, expanses of grass and tree-lined avenues. Green tells tales of life outdoors. Yet to use it indoors requires thought. Neutral green often has the effect of appearing rather washed out in an interior: it competes too much with the leaf green outdoors. Consequently, where there is a large surface area to cover, bright yellow greens or enigmatic blue-greens create better blends. For a bedroom, choose a quiet green, like a pistachio. Cool but not cold, refreshing but not suppressing, this kind of green is restful on the eye. A forest green works equally well, but needs quiet highlights to give this sombre hue an injection of life. Avoid yellow-greens or yellows in a bedroom as yellow communicates energy and vitality. Avocado bathrooms suites were the rage for Seventies bathrooms. Now considered unfashionable, this colour is actually perfect for bathers. A quiet, earthy green like this is known for its power to invigorate and refresh. Some shades of green don't reflect well on human skin so choosing the right green in a bathroom requires care. As green harmonizes with other colours found in nature, it looks eye-catching in a kitchen, particularly where granite, wood and stone are used for bench tops and work surfaces. Just take a look opposite, where the yellow-green mosaic tiling warmly counterbalances the chrome and white surfaces, bringing its hi-tech looks back to earth. Green is a colour that retreats. Unlike red, which jumps out, pale green recedes, which makes it perfect for playing with perceptions of space. A light green living room will look larger than life. Green's 'ready-to-go' association makes it the ideal colour for narrow areas like entrance ways, stairwells and hallways. In colour theory yellow-greens are stimulating, so employ these shades in places of activity. Ensure everyone can live with the hue you choose. After all, when we're seasick, we say we're feeling 'green'. Try painting test squares to find a colour everyone adores.

red

aubergine   kiss   blush   joy   sweet

All shades of red inject vitality. Consequently, reds are ideal for 'forgotten' spaces, such as a stairway, and exciting in functional areas, such as kitchens. For example, the coloured stripes in the hall (opposite, above left) and a deep red wall behind the staircase (opposite) bring lost spaces to life. Pink panelling in the kitchen (above) invokes appetite and activity.

67

Red ignites us. It is the colour that makes our hearts beat faster. It raises our metabolic rate and increases our pulses. The red family of hues is vibrant, stimulating and passionate. Magical powers are attributed to red: a small section of red-dyed yarn is sometimes seen in the middle of many Persian carpets to ward off the evil eye. In Chinese folklore, a front door painted red brings good fortune. In feng shui, red represents heat, laughter and good luck. When used in business, red brings wealth. And, when worn, red inspires leadership, confidence and personal power. On an emotional level, red represents anger, passion and love. Red unites extremes: it is warm and safe but also dangerous and daring. When we are angry, we 'see red'. It is the colour of revolution. And, it's the colour of embarrassment. It attracts, like red lipstick, or warns, like brake lights. Red is nature's exclamation mark: danger (poisonous berries) and passion (scarlet cheeks). Using powerful reds is not for the faint-hearted. Strong colours have an affinity with strong personalities. The home of the twentieth-century American acid-pen writer Dorothy Parker was completely decorated in pink, scarlet, vermilion, crimson, chestnut brown, rust, dark pink, rose red, red-brown and fuchsia – distinctive, passionate colours for an extremely distinctive personality. Internationally renowned fashion designer Matthew Williamson, king of colour, famously painted his boudoir in a striking hot pink, an ode to

India. In fact, in the Sixties *Vogue* Editor Diana Vreeland proclaimed hot pink the 'navy blue of India'. In the French romantic comedy *Amèlie*, red adorned every room of Amèlie's apartment. From maroon to toffee apple to rust, the red interior reflected the very essence of this hopeless romantic. Unlike blue, which retreats, red advances. It is the colour in the spectrum which catches our eye the most. It is the colour of romance, excitement and seduction. Think of bright red Saint Valentine's hearts and the wanton shades of the red-light district and 'scarlet' women. Interestingly, women name red as their favourite colour far more often than men. Variations of red have many of the same qualities as pure red. Orange unites the effects of red and yellow and creates warmth and wellbeing. It is a cheerful, radiant colour, full of energy, known in colour therapy as the hue that incites change. Pink is not simply red with a little white mixed in: it is a colour with a character all of its own and possesses many charms. Pink can be seductive, like magenta pink, or soft and maternal, like its underbelly, a sweet pale pink. Whatever the shade, all reds are colours that warm and stimulate us. Many people are shy of red. However, when applied with discretion, red is a home's lifeblood. In cold climates, red brings heat. In rooms for eating or cooking spaces, red stimulates the appetite, which is why red is the colour of choice for restaurants. Red signifies richness, luxury and decadence. So paint the town and your home red.

69

A bright red, softened with naturals, brings warmth.

'Reds transmit **passion**, vivacity, generosity. Pinks are curious colours. From the hues of the 'Pierre de Ronsard' rose to the shocking pink loved by Schiaparelli, these hues add a touch of **intrigue**.'

Rosita Missoni, fashion designer

71

Very pale pink paint on the wall, combined with white, is contemporary and romantic. It's soft, feminine and not too sugary. The hues provide a quiet backdrop, which is a canvas for a range of eclectic furniture.

73

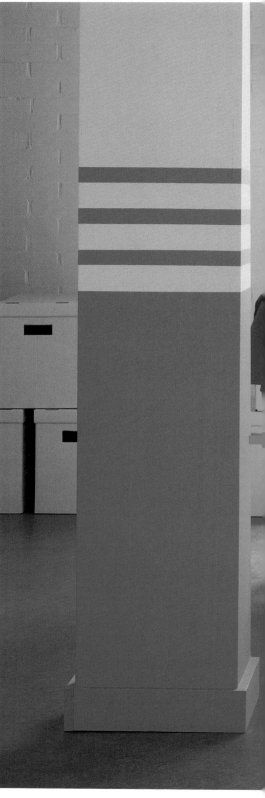

74

Red, orange and pink invigorate. Seen alone or together, these hues inspire, which makes them inspirational colleagues in the workplace. Balanced with white, these colours enliven any dull grey-beige office. Deep orange has been used on the notice board in the example above. The board creates a block of colour in the room, complemented by an office stool. The colour

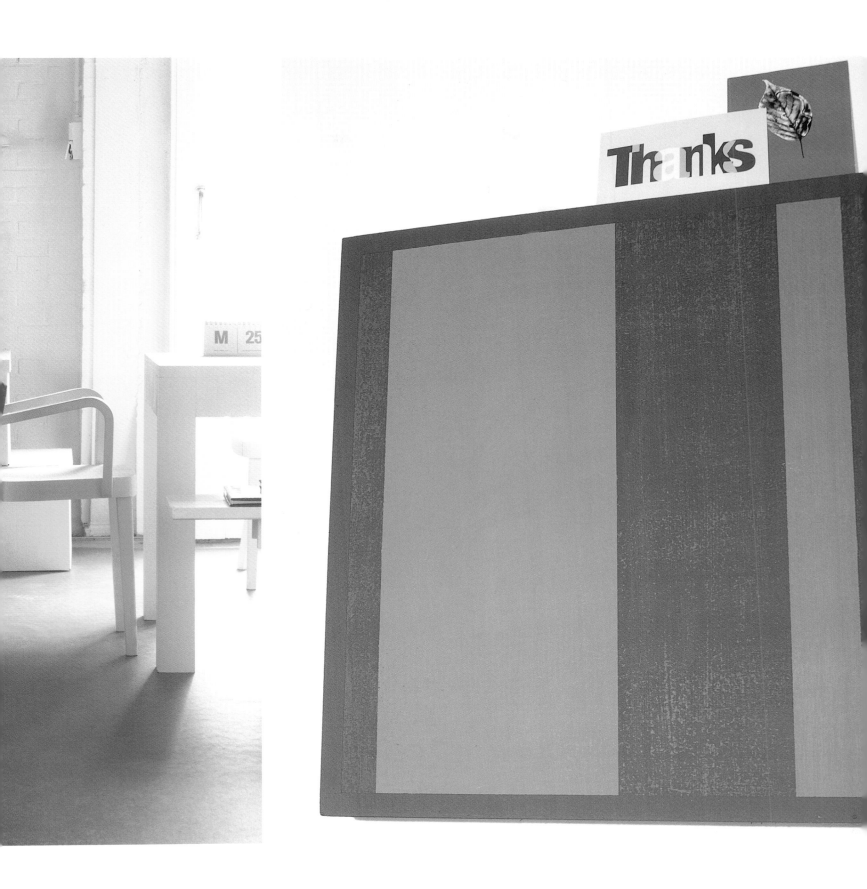

is echoed in a range of accessories. Bright orange allows the pillar to play a central role in an industrial space (centre) and unites the orange floor with the white ceiling. The canvas (right) shows how to brighten up a workspace simply with homemade artwork. This is the perfect example of how to add blocks of colour without painting a wall.

75

1 aubergine 2 lipstick 3 sun 4 sweet 5 joy 6 rust
7 cream 8 blossom 9 blush 10 terracotta 11 milk 12 kiss

Reds, from vermilion to dark burgundy, orange-blossom white to dark orange, and pale pink to bright fuchsia blend together, even if we have been taught that they clash. Red shimmers harmoniously with bright pink and orange. For a quieter environment, ensure there is plenty of white as a counterbalance or combine red with cooler, bluish reds and purples. Red and white is a classic duo. Just think of country-style gingham checks, calico or striped fabrics. Pink can be gentle and sweet, but becomes louder when combined with other reds or white. Highlights in complementary colours combine powerfully with reds: fuchsia and lime, red and green, orange and blue. Add purple for cool contrasts. If you just want to use red as a highlight, consider graphic effects, such as the figures stenciled in red, opposite.

77

Red is intense. However, it doesn't have to overpower a room. In this example, red has been used as an accent colour in a white room with a tomato-red armchair and a raspberry-red painted wall. While the room still exudes a calm, sober atmosphere, the red injects warmth and vitality. As this room shows, a little red is sometimes all it takes.

Red stimulates. So put it to good use. Combine reds together or let them stand alone. For example, a mélange of red, orange and bright pink is incredibly provocative. It's an exotic combination that ignores all the 'rules' about 'clashing colours'. If you need to soften the impact, combine red, pink and orange hues against a pale background, since you retain a balance as long as the reds are combined with white or natural colours. And if red makes you feel too daunted, just use a strong red, orange or pink on one wall. Paint it on in rooms where you go to re-energize. Or use it to stimulate activity, which makes it ideal for children's play areas. Red whets the appetite and motivates the chef in a kitchen. From walls painted red to rust Provencal-style floor tiles, red brings vibrancy into a room. If you're red-shy, accessorize. Buy an out-sized cherry red fridge or hang sturdy red pots from butchers' hooks. For dining rooms, use red to encourage conversation and a desire for vital victuals. Again, if painting the whole room is too overpowering, introduce a red table runner or apple-red napkins. In terms of optical illusions, red on walls make them look closer, and because of this, some designers advise against using it in small spaces. Yet ruby or a deep burgundy make a tiny space cosy and den-like, the perfect retreat on frosty winter nights. Firelight and candlelight brings reds to life. Orange is the warmest and most stimulating of all the 'reds'. It illuminates and energizes so is an ideal choice for home workspaces. Colour therapists extol it as a colour of change. If you're feeling inert, at a crossroads, try a little of it in your home for inspiration. Reds can also be subtle, like pink, certainly not limited to little girls' bedrooms. Strong, sophisticated and feminine, pink also looks soft and modern in a living room. In the bathroom, a subtle pink reassures, providing a visual embrace. Pale pink is a tonic for tired minds and bodies. And red also lends itself to graphic effects with paint. For example, in the picture opposite, an ordinary hallway is instantly transformed.

multicolour

| kiss | blush | joy | twilight | dream |
| fresh | moon | sun | spring | star |

As design rebel Verner Panton extolled, the use of colour is limited only by your imagination. And, with paint, you can add to the mix any colour you desire. The floor in the child's bedroom (opposite, centre top) is a bright candy pink. However, don't limit paint to large floors or walls. Use it to revitalize and add vibrant shades to furniture, like the born-again chair (above right).

85

Life is never monochrome. Colour is everywhere, coming in so many combinations. In nature, colours are never predictable. A meadow full of wild flowers or a market with dozens of colours is not made up of hues from a carefully arranged colour chart but is, instead, a melting pot of all imaginable and unimaginable colours simultaneously. In the past decades, multicolour has left its colourful imprint. After the dark days of the Second World War, the Sixties rebelled in psychedelic colours with wild and crazy patterns of deep purple, lime greens, lurid reds and bright blues. Design, at last, like the Sixties, was swinging. The colour revolutionary of the time, Danish designer Verner Panton, celebrated colour combinations in his maverick interiors. Other epochs, like the lavish, garish interiors of Indian maharajahs or the glitzy palaces of Louis XIV, the indulgent Sun King, have also celebrated the glory of colour. Vincent Van Gogh's bedroom echoed his deep love for myriad colours. In a letter to his brother Theo, he described it: 'The walls are pale violet. The floor is of red tile. The wood of the bed and chairs is the yellow of fresh butter, the sheet and pillows very light lemon green. The coverlet scarlet. The window green. The toilet table orange…' As natural environments have no strict pattern of colour, an interior with many colours like Van Gogh's bedroom is effortless and spontaneous. A multicoloured home is a celebration of beauty, a form of self-expression. In some ways it is

86

child-like, reminiscent of confectionery, confetti, fizzy drinks, a box of coloured crayons, or a pile of school folders. Multicolour is where our imagination runs riot. However, a multicoloured interior does not have to look immature. It can sparkle like a starlit night or burst forth like a firework display and it can glow like shards of light from a church's stained-glass window. Yet multicolour is also as refined as a seventeenth-century still life or as elegant as a French chateau. Multicolour exists in many forms. Look for inspiration in daily life. A flower garden shows off bright, springtime colours. An Indian market displays a range of coloured spices , neatly presented in pyramids of turmeric, saffron, cayenne, cumin and paprika. Or, take inspiration from foreign climes. Consider for example, the saturated, bright colours of India where red, orange, bright pink, dark blue and apple green are used alongside each other. Or, Cézanne's Provence in France, with its combinations of lavender, salmon pink and sunflower yellow. Mexico's colours follow the lead of its legendary architect, Luis Barragán, who used soft pinks, bold blues, fresh aqua greens and turquoise. Many of these combinations have a different effect in higher latitudes simply because the light appears cooler. For example, in the English winter, the light is one-tenth of its high summer intensity. If a set of exotic colours strike you, alter the shades to suit the light. Follow the lead of Panton and unchain your colour palette. Let it go wild.

Multicolour has a sense of humour. Blocks of complementary colours on the wall (left) provide a sense of fun in this playful living room. While multicolour is about experimenting with a multitude of shades, it is also about emphasizing pattern, illustrated by the storage baskets (right).

'Some people imagine that **colour** is tiring to live with, forgetting how dreary it is to sit in dull rooms without a spark of interest to **stimulate** the eye.'

Trisha Guild, from *Trisha Guild on Colour*

Multicoloured interiors can also be muted and atmospheric, as in this light-filled family house. A pale pinewood floor has been complemented with the warm, fruity colours of the cushions, lampshades, rugs and blinds. As a backdrop, a fresh light blue adorns the wall.

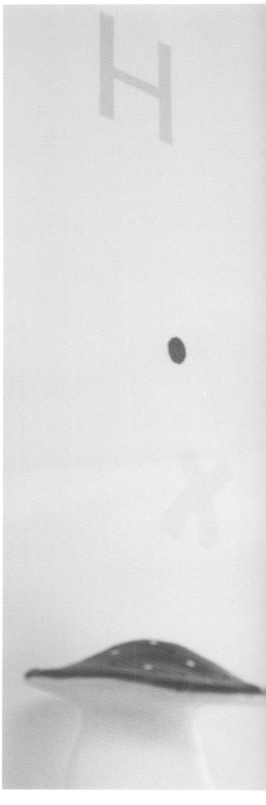

Paint has created a happy-go-lucky mood throughout this house in different ways. The chairs in the dining room (above left) are all the same design but each has been painted in a different colour: purple, light blue, red, pink and light lime. A dusky blue adorns the wall. While a wall in the children's bedroom (centre) has been given a playful highlight of colour with letters

painted in grey, red, light blue and mauve. Bright colours, right down to the fabric for the floor cushion, have been chosen for a seating area (above right). To keep this bold scheme from being too lurid, pale pinewood furniture and a fresh white backdrop work together to ground the bright colours. Accessories in more subtle shades can soften the look.

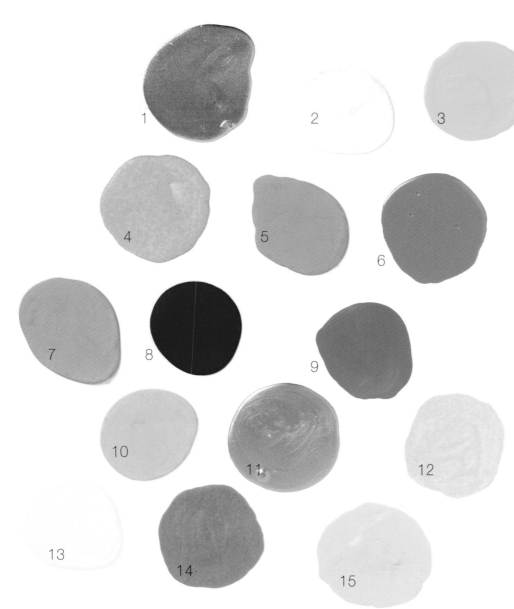

1 moon 2 milk 3 sand 4 sunflower 5 twilight 6 blush
7 dream 8 kiss 9 sky 10 fresh 11 sun 12 eggshell
13 cream 14 joy 15 chalk

No laws govern a multicoloured interior: anything is possible. You are the painter. Even so, there are still a few rules of thumb worth keeping in mind. If you are employing many colours together, remember a chaotic mix always look best against a canvas of white or natural shades. Keep colours within one tone: all intense, dark velvety colours, or all of a similar lightness. Full of charisma, the children's corner of a living room, illustrated right, looks like a place to play. The wall has been painted bright blue to contrast with the red table and the toys. Multicolour is often used for children's spaces but, other interiors in this chapter show how multicolour can work well in most rooms. Stylish and sophisticated, there's absolutely no reason to give multicolour an age limit. After all, everyone needs to express their *joie de vivre*.

95

A multicoloured interior is whatever it chooses to be. It is not tied to a particular style or mood. Make it romantic, reminiscent of a posy of flowers. Or, emulate the exotic riot of colours of an Indian street scene. While multicolour is playful, it is equally refined and can be elegant and traditional like an early nineteenth-century house upholstered in rich damask and velvet, with deep, plush walls. It also works well with the minimal design of a modern interior as long as the colours are kept under control – a white backdrop is the perfect foil. Minimalist design is a sound foundation for an explosion of colour: take, for example, a neat row of chairs of the same design but in different colours, or a band of coloured stripes, illustrated right, which bring warmth and life to a stark room. With multicolour, you don't have to use every colour in the rainbow: just imagine a contrasting combination of two main colours, such as fuchsia and lime, or complementary colours, such as blue and orange, supported by colourful accents elsewhere. Or choose families of colours, such as those of exotic fruits or spices. In terms of application, take a good look at the room. Use it to highlight off-beat elements like a curved wall or add stripes to bring a recessed alcove to life. Multicolour has the power to change perceptions of space. To 'enlarge' a room, paint a dark colour up to chest height, finishing with a contrasting stripe, and paint the rest of the room up to the ceiling in a lighter colour. Finish off by coating the ceiling in a bright white and – magic! – the room looks taller. As a floor is one of a room's largest surfaces, if you paint it in a bold colour, you'll draw attention to its width. And, if you paint the skirting board with the same colour, the floor will look even wider. Multicolour is a clever way to create visual surprises, particularly in unloved spaces, like hallways and passageways. A set of colourful horizontal stripes moving down the wall of a hallway makes it a destination, rather than just part of the journey.

black-white-grey

slate

taupe

dew

pearl

cream

Black, white and all the greys in between make a house timeless. Greys suit any interior style.
Its many shades are demonstrated in the dark slate used for the wall behind the candlesticks
(opposite, above left), the staircase stained ebony black (opposite, below left), the cabinet in
the living room (above left) and the dew grey in the bathroom (below right).

101

Black, white and grey are not strictly colours. They live beyond the colour spectrum. Yet this elegant trio adds depth to any interior. Bright, clean white is the bedrock for all interiors, while black is its ultimate contrast. Together the two are light and shade, reticence and dominance, traditionalism and modernism. Black on white has become an eternal standard: black tuxedos with white shirts, fine lace collars over black velvet, the luminescent moon in a night sky, the stark, grainy realism of black-and-white photographs,the chequered floors of an Art Deco kitchen. The Modernists celebrated this duo, inspired by painters of the time, like the studies of blocks and grids of Piet Mondrian. Famed architect Le Corbusier contrasted his black leather-and-chrome furniture against a white background, moving from a crisp, white Cubist period to a concrete, industrial-style after the Second World War. 'Architecture,' he remarked, 'is the masterly, correct and magnificent play of masses bought together in light.' For him, light and shadow or black, white and the shades grey between, bought buildings to life. Another quietly brilliant designer of the period, Eileen Gray, created beautifully elegant interiors with bold strokes of black and white, all shot with greys. Her interior for client Susan Talbot featured over-sized zebra skins, Gray's own coiled white 'Bibendum' chairs and black-lacquered accessories. This pair has no pretensions; it is too extremes united. The Chinese are reticent about using black and white as both are associated with death. The interplay between them is summed up by 'yin and yang', a symbol depicting how the colours are entwined in an eternal struggle for power, yet are mutually dependent like the male and female energies they represent. There are as many shades of black as there are of white. Van Gogh identified 28 shades of black in the paintings of Dutch painter Franz Hals. Grey softens both colours. And, when the endless variants of these two colours collide, they produce a diverse range of grey, a soft hue seen in the tranquil calm before dusk. Grey, placed between two strong colours, softens both. But grey is not purely and simply neutral. Grey is tasteful, luxurious and comforting. The gentle greys of a calm sea, of cloudy skies, of motionless mist, give us a comfortable feeling of wellbeing that we can emulate in our interiors. We know that white is the foundation for interiors, but some surfaces can also be replaced by subtle misty tones of grey, a strong slate or clay grey. Grey quietens bright colours and is especially stylish when combined with black and white or natural tones, like tweed, woods and celadon. What's more, black, white and grey are excellent colours to experiment with in creating graphic design effects, such as stripes, shapes and blocks of colour. Create classic modernist lines or marry the colour trio with chrome for a hi-tech contemporary look. Use black and white for powerful visual contrasts and add grey to create a gentle, timeless elegance.

Walls painted in a dewy grey and milky white.

'Grey and the deeper shades of charcoal and black have **integrity** of their own. The myriad of moods conveyed in black, grey and white are endless and **timeless** whether sophisticated or austere.'

John Rocha, fashion designer

A room decorated in natural colours creates a calm, modern feel when different tones of greys are used. The grey on the wall demonstrates how grey can be warm and earthy, particularly with natural wood.

107

Black, white and grey are used widely in work environments and have associations with dull, suffocating offices. The examples above demonstrate how this trio can make a workspace warm, inviting and studio-like. A tiled floor effect is shown in the room (left), painted in high-gloss black and white. The wall (centre) painted a dark, warm grey has been magically

transformed into a gigantic calendar with magnets to hold memos in place. The attic room (right) has been lightened up with a chalky white on the wall and a creamy white on the woodwork, while the floor has been painted in dark, stylish slate. A chrome chair injects mid-tones of silvery grey. This almost stark black-and-white study still manages to look informal and inviting.

109

1 slate 2 dew 3 oyster 4 milk 5 cream 6 stone
7 charcoal 8 pearl 9 dove 10 cloud

The possibilities are infinite for combinations of black, white and grey. Black and white is such a classic combination that wherever it resides it gives a touch of sophistication. A black floor in a white interior is timeless. Black on the wall is a bold venture, but if used on just one wall it can be effective, as long as the other walls are left white. Black and white can be softened and enlivened with innumerable shades of grey, from dark slate to the pale warmth of pearl grey or the cool lightness of a dewy grey. Grey can be a substitute for white. It makes a good background for bright colours and combines subtly with natural tones. Grey is well suited to creative, striking two-tone effects, illustrated opposite: the clocks have been mounted on a slate-grey background, while below, the wall has been painted in a soft stone grey.

111

Black has power. It makes white whiter and makes colours more pronounced. Although black appears to be just one colour, there are dozens of variations: the dense jet black and ebony against blacks with a hue, such as dark grey anthracite, blue-grey slate and an intense bluish ink black. Certainly, black works well in graphic designs when combined with white: a black frame helps a print stand out from the wall, and black defines the design of a piece of furniture. Angular objects and dark types of wood help display black to its best advantage (a charcoal tone or blue-grey black is eye-catching and on woodwork or wood floors). In a living room, large pieces of sculptural furniture are beautiful in black. For an effect less defined by contrast, there is grey. All possible shades of grey reside on a sliding scale between black and white. Pure grey is neutral. For a calm, soothing space, a soft pale dewy grey, contrasted with a clean white, is the perfect colour for bathrooms. When we're in a flat mood, we say we're having a 'grey day' so steer clear of deadpan greys in bedrooms, or other places where we rest and revive. Choose instead warm pinky greys that combine beautifully with the fresh whites of newly laundered linens. Together, whites, greys and natural colours make for a good combination in modern interiors. However, far from being too formal, the use of dark or lime-washed wood with warmer shades of grey provides a comfortable, earthy feel. A black-white-grey interior is timeless and stylish, particularly when you play with different textures like smooth and rough, and matt and gloss. Matt charcoal creates a very different effect from glossy jet black, while a matt, milk-white wall contrasts well with smooth white porcelain. In the room opposite, there are endless shades of grey balanced with warm wood tones and white. The blackboard in the hall is a great way to introduce a grey tone to a house. For contrast, the walls have been painted in oyster white and the mirror frame in a milky white. It is more subtle than a black-and-white contrast but equally as powerful.

7

naturals

granite

aubergine

october

oyster

natural

Natural colours possess a sense of quiet elegance, calm and unity. Cool and warm, traditional and modern, rustic and urban, naturals are all part of the same palette, which is why they combine so harmoniously. Yet within the palette there are so many different looks. For contrast, team natural colours with its material cousins like leather, wood, linen, stone and earthenware.

117

Stone, sand and clay. Slate, pebble and ochre. Nut brown, burnt sienna and rosehip. Just saying the names of natural colours makes us aware of the reason we love these hues so much. When we visualize them, we almost smell their aromas. Think of biscuit, plum, aubergine, walnut and oatmeal. These hues simply remind us of our deep, primal connection with the earth. These are the colours of clay, of raw nature, of stone, cane, terracotta and tree trunks. These are colours that are earthy or elegant, subtle or dominant, gentle or rough. They can dress a home in rustic simplicity or modernist chic. Naturals are never excessively eye-catching or obtrusive. Even the strongest tones are easy to live with. The deeper tones of these are now often sold as 'heritage' paints, colours from the Georgian and Victorian eras, where a palette of deep naturals like warm terracottas, plum reds and chocolate browns adorned interiors. The lighter tones like mushroom, taupe and sandstone, have recently become more popular in colour charts. These shades have become the antidote to the break-neck speed of modern life, rediscovered in the 'honest' peeled-back, pared-down Nineties. As society becomes obsessed with a 24/7 lifestyle, it's no wonder we long to be reminded of rural tranquillity, with its sweeping organic lines and natural palette. At the beginning of the twentieth century, after the industrial revolution had put life on fast-forward with reforms in technology, Art Nouveau stormed into design with a similar backlash. It extolled nature's virtues with sensuous, organic flowing lines, stylized plant designs and down-to-earth colours, like apricots, tans and emerald greens. As seen in these beautiful, swirling designs, natural colours combine seamlessly and effortlessly. Within naturals are so many colours, cool and warm, light and dark. To add visual texture, experiment with nature's materials. Think coarse-woven linen, soft fur, shells, old lace, hemp, coconut matting on a wood floor, wicker baskets and pebbles. Decorate by instinct. We have a natural affinity with certain colours. Browns are ideal for floors because of their earthiness: they literally ground us. Dark chocolate embodies a deep sense of richness and warmth, like a mug of piping hot cocoa. Shades of cream create a touch of elegance and style while faded naturals cater for a somewhat cooler effect. And we feel warmed by the soft shades of terracotta, or 'fired earth'. In general, cool naturals look more modern than warmer tones and are suited to contemporary interiors because they marry beautifully with steel, greys and pale wood floors. Warmer naturals combine with cream and ecru in a more traditional interior. Naturally coarse materials, such as coconut matting, wood floors, hemp and stone, create a rustic feel. So bring the beauty of the outdoors indoors and bring your fast-paced life back down to earth. As writer Ralph Waldo Emerson said: 'Nature always wears the colours of the spirit.'

A milky white provides a soft canvas.

'I am addicted to taupe. For me, naturals are easy to live with and low-key. They feel **protective**. I'd contrast taupe with purples and reds.'

Kelly Hoppen, interior designer

White and naturals are the perfect duo for time-pressed urbanites. In this modern rustic living room, a white canvas is interrupted by a warm wood floor, a pine table, and black and dark brown details.

123

Dark natural colours provide a room with visual fullstops. In the living room (left), dark contrasts give more depth to the main theme of off-white by distinctive lamps with sculptural wooden bases and smooth wood tables. The entrance hall (centre) displays an intriguing interplay between light and dark naturals, illustrated in the dark tiled floor, the stair treads,

the banister railing and the picture frames. All the woodwork has been painted in light cream and the wall a grey-brown oyster. The terracotta tiles on the floor add a sense of warmth and vitality. In the room (right) a pale khaki tint has been added to the dominant themes of white and cream. Here the dark wood of the chair legs invokes a sense of depth and drama.

1 oyster 2 coffee 3 milk 4 powder 5 natural 6 wheat
7 sandstone 8 aubergine 9 cream 10 pearl
11 june 12 october

Warm naturals are shades of gold, ivory white, terracotta, copper and reddish browns that recall the autumn season, hearth fires and fallen leaves. The cooler side of the palette contains sandstone, taupe, dark wenge, chocolate brown, mushroom grey and stormy greys that have a more wintry effect. Naturals combine well together or serve as the foundation for stronger colours. Cool naturals look good in modern interiors because they complement steel, all shades of grey and pale wood flooring. Warmer naturals combine well with creamy tones in a more traditional interior. See the variety of warmth and texture in stained wood in the workspace opposite, where the wood stain creates a captivating display of natural colours (ebony, mahogany, chestnut and pine woods). The look is sensuous and sumptuous.

127

Naturals achieve an elegant, welcoming effect in combination with creamy whites, comfortable furniture, luxurious materials and a juxtaposition of coarse and matt textures contrasted with shiny, glossy surfaces.

Naturals suggest space and calm. They speak to us of the great outdoors, of days by a quiet river or a ramble through autumnal woods. Be careful when choosing an all-natural palette however, as some shades may be too subdued. Despite their natural ability to harmonize, they can look almost colourless. To overcome this visual monotony, play with tone and structure. Set creamy colours against strong, dark colours, such as chocolate or aubergine. Or, take a mushroom-coloured living room and bring it to life with dark woods, like wenge, and fresh, breezy whites. The mood suggested by, for example, cream with pale wood is determined to a great extent by materials and their texture. If you choose materials such as coconut matting, reclaimed wood floors, rough linen weaves and unfinished stone or raw wood, the result is raw and rustic. However, you can see in the kitchen opposite that the effect of off-white and wood looks sleek, sophisticated and contemporary with smooth, polished lines. This feel comes from the shiny surfaces and the wood veneer, combined with gleaming chrome, a smooth, stone-tile floor and chic contemporary details. The pale wood makes the kitchen look welcoming despite all its shining perfection. In a hi-tech utilitarian kitchen like this one, naturals produce a softening effect. Use naturals to soften hard looks in almost any room of the house. In a bedroom, earthy colours are perfect for relaxing the senses. Imagine a room with taupe on the walls, a sheepskin rug underfoot, thick grey felt curtains and a generously large bed covered with fresh silk sheets, a nutmeg-coloured mohair blanket and extra-soft duck-feather pillows dressed with lavender-scented linens. Just as natural colours are easy on the eye, they are restful to our minds and bodies. As you'd expect, nature's hues look quietly stunning in bathrooms. Wicker storage baskets, unpainted wooden shelves, sea sponges, driftwood, beach pebbles and even a sweet-scented cedar wood Japanese-style squat bath bring with them nature and all its restorative powers.

pastels

aubergine

oyster

serenity

sea

mist

sweet

cream

milk

Pastels don't need to be sugary. Counterbalanced by naturals, they are quietly vibrant. See how pastels work in the pale green dining area set against dark wood (far left); in the sea green walls with lime-coloured eggcups (opposite below); and in a pale mauve behind rustic garden chairs (left). A pale-lilac pastel throw and candy pink cushion liven up a white sofa (above).

135

Pink ballet shoes, frosting on cakes, marshmallows, baby-blue mittens, bridesmaids' dresses: pastel hues evoke images of sweetness and innocence. They remind us of everything that is fresh and new, like spring flowers and apple blossom, sweet and sugary, like sorbets and milkshakes. Pastels are relaxing, refreshing, gentle and optimistic. They are every colour in the rainbow with a touch of white. There is a whole wardrobe of pastels to choose from: cool or warm, sweet or fresh, bright or pale. Feminine or 'girlie' pastels and florals are increasingly popular interior choices. Their child-like optimism is the perfect antidote for turbulent times. This recent fashion has retro roots. The optimistic Fifties embraced the innocent charm of pastels. Lemon yellows, pale pinks and baby blues graced everything from egg beaters and toasters to Vespas. Melamine, a laminate like Formica, became the Fifties housewife's byword for chic, as a low cost, durable, work surface for kitchens that came in a variety of pastel shades. Yet, in modern life, we frequently relegate pastels to little girls' or babies' bedrooms. However, pastels can be sophisticated. A room decorated in pastels can look fresh and modern, or sumptuous and elegant or, in contrast, subtle and natural. A room can become charming and spring-like with pale pink, buttercup yellow, linden green and the colours of old-fashioned roses and sweet peas. Ice-cream colours are fresh and more contemporary: cool colours diluted with white, such as pistachio, pale lemon, tangerine and cool pink. If pastels are given a touch of grey, but still appear as strong colours, they recall the glamorous opulence of palaces from the eighteenth through to the early twentieth centuries. The delicate shades of old rose, champagne, blue-green, ivory, coral, lavender, grey-green and shell pink have a timeless quality. These hues evoke glamorous ballroom scenes from historical movies: silk stockings, shining satin cushions, embroidered Chinese draperies and lavish boudoirs. Or think of Louis XV's wife, Madame de Pompadour, and her French boudoir, in pinks, pale yellows and powder blues. These colours now look contemporary. For example, combining lilac with pale turquoise or mauve with sea green can look very chic. Add a touch of grey to a shade of pastel and it becomes exceptionally restrained and subtle. These soft pastels are colours barely suggested, like the indefinable colour of the underside of rosemary leaves, of pearls or mist. It is very simple to prevent pastels from becoming too sugary. Even if you are crazy about lemon yellow and pink, they don't need to be saccharine. Using pastels with white or more dominant colours and with smooth or coarse textures gives these striking colours a contemporary look. For example, lilac and purple also go well with naturals: dark brown with pale pink or baby blue, taupe with lilac. Whatever hue of pastel you choose, the result is always liberating.

On the wall is a quiet serene green.

'Soothing, **calming**, forgiving, **restful**, – these are feelings I associate with pastels. I like to team pastels with highlights in stronger darker colours. Mixing mint with chocolate brown, duck-egg blue with aubergine equals **sophistication** and glamour'

Andrea Lynch,
Art Director of *Elle Decoration*

A painted dado effect, with light creamy yellow below and a cooler, water-colour pastel above. The bright, powdery white used for the dado rail itself makes the room seem wider than it really is.

Pastels can be used to striking effect, as in these three different rooms. In the hall (left) the cool, neutral colours of milk and grey are interrupted by a pink throw resting casually on a chair. Use materials like this to give a light, gentle touch to an otherwise hard-edged interior. See just how minimal, modern and playful pastels can be: the wall (centre) is striped with fresh

green, clay, peach, pale blue and dark grey. In the living room (right) one wall is painted lemon yellow, which brings in a feeling of sunshine and light. Plenty of white and a splash of grey softens the look. In all three rooms, the result is not at all sugary but fresh and contemporary. By harmonizing with naturals, each scheme discovers its own equilibrium.

143

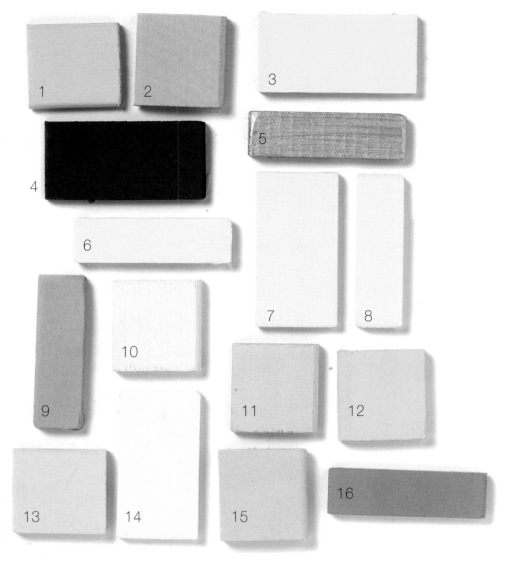

1 sorbet 2 sea 3 star 4 aubergine 5 moon
6 blossom 7 sweet 8 powder 9 oyster 10 milk
11 lemon 12 water 13 mist 14 cream 15 pearl
16 serenity

The way to temper the sweetness of pastels is to mix them with contrasting shades. Use a fresh white or a deep natural colour like aubergine to tone them down. Greyish pastels are also good with cooler, strong colours. Also, a modern interior in pastels works well with a minimalist design. While pastels need heavy accents to give them depth, remember to keep them light with the airiness of white or soft, cool greys. To breathe life into the whole look, accessorize with glass, chrome and reflective surfaces rather than heavy, chunky furniture and details, like black leather sofas or heavy earthenware. Try to opt for a no-frills approach, eschewing floral fabrics or lace to prevent the look becoming too feminine. The living room opposite shows light purple combining beautifully with naked wood and a white sofa.

145

Remember how pastel-coloured shirts suddenly became terribly macho when worn by the heroes from the TV series *Miami Vice*? The taboo on these kinds of subtle colours in men's fashions disappeared in one episode. The same shift in thinking now applies to interiors. Until recently, the traditional domain for pastels were childrens' rooms, and quiet, 'feminine' spaces. Surprisingly, these colours are now making an appearance in the functional rooms of the home. For example, you can see an unexpected use of pastels in this kitchen, opposite, with an otherwise relatively formal and functional layout. To counter this, the wall above the work surface has been painted a purple-blue. Retro Fifties looks are also increasingly popular in the kitchen, with candy-coloured stools and retro-style accessories, like manufacturer Smeg's fridges in pink, baby blue and mint green. These pastel pieces are timeless classics and work well to soften the industrial workshop feel of a kitchen. Colourful laminates, floral tea towels and melamine reproduction tableware also introduce a retro feel. Lemon yellow brings light, energy and quiet zing into a sunless kitchen. It is no surprise that pastels provide a refreshing, restful feel in a bedroom. Their delicate shades radiate a subtle energy. Candy pinks, minty greens or pale blues make fresh, invigorating backdrops to white linens or pockets of patterned fabrics like paisley. In the bathroom, pastels are easy on the eye. Lilac or lavender calms, rests and reassures, and as these colours are all tinted with white, they are expansive and make any small space look larger. Living rooms demand an easy colour. Here, the neutral shades of pastels work best, like milky coffees and champagnes. Pastels are also effective in often ignored areas, like stairwells and hallways. Add a sense of playfulness to these unloved spaces with candy colours. However, pastels have been lavished on nurseries and children's bedrooms for a good reason. Indulge them. Paint their rooms in peppermint and chocolate chip or marshmallow pink.

gloss and glitter

sun   moon   gleam

Gloss and matt paint prove that opposites attract. The wall behind the mantelpiece (far left, above) has been painted in stripes of ultra matt. Silvery circles (far left, below) are details that bring in a touch of decadence. Indulgent dining tables have always been adorned in gold trimmings, which is why the table (above) looks inviting, covered in its glorious, lacy gold cloth.

151

Gloss and glitter provide shine and shimmer. Imagine a red velvet cushion. Now picture a shiny, red Ferrari. It's the same red, but each one feels completely different. Compare a matt-white plastered wall with a gleaming gold-painted wall. Gloss and glitter appeal to our sense of touch. From the rich, vibrant glow of silver and gold to the enigmatic glimmer of mother-of-pearl, the glitter of glass and crystal to the high gloss of a lacquered Chinese cabinet, the clear reflection of gilt-framed mirrors to the warm patina of wood veneer and leather, gloss and glitter gives depth and breadth. Gold and silver are an example of gloss and glitter, containing an in-built sheen. Throughout history these colours have signified opulence and exalted those who have touched them. From the Hall of Mirrors in Louis XIV's palace at Versailles in France to the gold hieroglyphics of Ancient Egyptian temples, gold and silver have been associated with the colours of kings and queens, emperors and high priests. Strict rules precluding commoners from wearing gold, dominated many royal courts. Legend tells that Cleopatra used gold and silver to seduce Julius Caesar. She sailed up on a barge with billowing purple sails, powered by silver oars, and lay, dressed as Aphrodite under a gold-embroidered awning. In Medieval art, gold was a holy, heavenly colour. Through the ages gold has stood as a symbol of wealth and sumptuousness. More recently, gold, red and black were the colours of the Eighties, a statement of a decade of indulgence and excess. Gold's sheen has lost none of its glamour: a gilt frame or stitch of gold embroidery is all it takes to pay homage to the allure of gold. Silver is gold's quiet second cousin. From the warmth of antique silver to the cool gleam of modern chrome, silver brings with it sheen and shimmer. Luckily, wall paint is now available in gold and silver. Bring vivacity and glamour into you interior by painting just one wall. However, a shimmery allure is not reserved for silver and gold alone. Add it to existing paint colours, or give any wall colour an enigmatic, sparkle by applying a coat of transparent, glittering mother-of-pearl paint on top. Depending on the type of light, this can transform a room's brightness. Naturally, all of this glossiness and glitter works best if contrasted with matt and coarser surfaces. For example, a monochrome interior of blacks, whites and greys acquires depth by adding varying textures of matt and gloss. To give textural paints extra sensuality, team them with luxurious, indulgent fabrics and materials, such as velvet, silk or fur. Aside from gloss and glittery paints, there are also varieties that are ultra matt or exhibit a subtle, rougher surface, such as stucco-texture paint for a rough, plastered effect or sand paint with a fine, grainy finish. Textured paints enrich the natural beauty of neutral colours. With an ultra matt background, the perfect contrast is anything that glitters. Glam up your interior. After all, you are king of your own castle.

Gold-coloured paint on
a sliding partition wall.

'I like this word **decadent**; all shimmering with purple and gold.'

Paul Verlaine, poet and philosopher

156 Gold and silver is now also available in one-litre wall paint containers, the perfect amount for experimenting on small areas and details in matt and gloss. The stairwell (left) has been painted in a checkerboard pattern of contrasting squares in a grey-white and aubergine. The effect is spectacular. Gold, silver and gloss are seen in the details in the living room (centre).

The whole look is luxurious, from the silvery sheen of the chair's upholstery and a canvas painted in glittery gold, to a glossy lampshade with gold lining and a frothy cushion for contrast. In the workspace (right) a silver band has been painted across a matt white wall to form the canvas for a series of photographs. The glossy table reflects the light and enhances the space.

157

1 moon 2 gleam 3 sun

Go for gold. Now hues of gold, silver and mother-of-pearl give you the opportunity to bring glamour and glitter into your home. Gold is warming on a wall, especially in combination with creamy colours or royal reds and it is subtle when mixed with pale shades of green and chalky browns. Gold with blue is an ode to kings and queens, while silver with blue is fairytale-like. Silver with greys and pastels is elegant, particularly in combination with delicate, shiny materials, such as silk and satin. Finally, silver with purple has an imperial grandeur, illustrated in the living room, right. Here you see the hallway, painted in silver, from the perspective of the living room with its aubergine walls and glossy white woodwork. A transparent mother-of-pearl gloss gives an enigmatic shimmer across any type of wall paint.

Glossiness and glitter lend a movie-star allure to our homes. Use it anywhere, even in the bathroom, but if there is one room in the home that is tailor-made for the regal, indulgent effect of gloss and glitter it's the bedroom. The walls in the bedroom opposite, have been painted in a matt powder blue, a cool, enigmatic colour. Alternate squares have been painted over in a mother-of-pearl gloss, which sparkle and shine in the lamplight. Furthermore, the entire content of the bedroom adds to the indulgent atmosphere. There is a subtle interplay between glossy, sparkling, matt and textured surfaces. The second chief colour, brilliant white, makes the room luxuriously airy. The chandelier reflects a dazzling light, the cushions are covered in rich, shiny fabrics, and the frothy woven rug, a small extravagance for bare feet, contrasts with the smooth floor.

162 View the quiet brilliance of an interior with an ultra matt finish. A dado has been painted in an oyster white. To give the colour weight, the paint has been applied in wide arcs using a wide, straight-edged brush. Above the dado, the wall painted white creates textural variation.

Combine rough with smooth, black with white, gloss with glitter. Create a wall that will make you want to touch it. All you need to do is apply textured paint in different ways. Paint it on in rough strokes, giving the texture a pattern, or roll it on smoothly. Textured paint versions of oyster white and powder have been used in the rooms opposite. With their velvety, sandy sheen, these soft colours come alive. Use gloss in any room in the house that needs light. Its reflective nature helps sunlight bounce around a room, giving it the illusion of space. To create new horizons and a luxurious sense of space in any room, simply team a pale glossy surface with an over-sized shiny, gilt-edged mirror. In kitchens where shiny surfaces abound, simply keep the background matt to create contrast and highlights. The sheen of stainless-steel sinks and shiny chrome door handles tend to stand out against a matt white backdrop. To give kitchens their own glamour, hang gleaming utensils, like shiny woks, polished colanders, and copper pots from butchers' hooks. Dining rooms have always been an ode to decadence. In grand houses of the past, vast arrays of silver vessels, crystal and gold-gilded plates were simply piled on tables as a testament to wealth and magnificence. To emphasize your own collection, display pieces on a fine weave linen table cloth. A wall of gold in any formal dining room, crowned with a chandelier, makes the whole room indulgent. To prevent it from seeming too extravagant, tone it down with natural materials like dark wood seats and sensible cream linens. Living rooms with gold also sparkle. If lavishing gold on the walls seems too flamboyant, let it shine in small doses by painting chair legs or picture frames. Where gold reflects the sun and daylight, silver mirrors the moon and the night. Silver gives a bedroom a feeling of romance, which as writer Amanda Cross says, becomes 'the glamour which turns the dust of everyday life into a golden haze.' With silver glittering on the walls, bedrooms become boudoirs, places for starry-eyed dreams.

10

colour in practice

CHOOSING COLOURS

Celebrate colour. From subtle shades and quiet pastels to luxurious golds and sophisticated black on white, it's time to liberate your inner colours and unleash them into your living space. Unsure of what you actually like? Well, it's time to get inspired. Once you become aware of colour, you'll notice how it's the first thing that shapes your response to the world around you. Take a walk through the woods and notice a thousand of shades of green and see how colours shimmer and change. Van Gogh observed how many colours the sea possessed. 'The Mediterranean has the colour of mackerel,' he wrote. 'You don't always know if it is green or violet, you can't even say it's blue, because the next moment the changing reflection has taken on a tint of rose or grey.'

Colours are everywhere in different nuances and shades. Once you've taken stock of the colours in your environment, make a mental checklist of the colours you already live with. As Bauhaus artist Johannes Itten showed in his studies, most of us already have a colour palette we identify with. Think about the style and colours of your favourite clothes, shoes, bags and then look at how your personal style is expressed in your home, in your furniture, paintings and accessories.

Choosing a colour is part intuition, part practicality. When considering a colour for a room, think about what the room needs and what you use it for. Is it formal or inviting? Is the room pint-sized or too big? How much light does it receive? Does it remind you of a particular era? It's also about your imagination. Do you love an epoch, say the buzz of the Eighties or the swing of the Sixties? Or are you drawn to a place? The brassy colours of India? The fresh, bright hues of Mexico?

Sometimes it's hard to imagine what effect colours will have in your home, so it can be useful to understand a little bit more about how they work – when it comes to choosing colours, there are a few rules of thumb. Like all 'rules' it's useful to know what they are, then learn how to break them. In the end, the only thing that counts is what you love.

Help yourself decide

To assist you in your choice of colour, think about the following:

- The size of the walls, floors or objects that you wish to colour
- The function of the surface
- The texture of the surface
- The shape of the surface
- The kind of material you'll be painting on
- The light conditions

Now take a paper and pen and answer the following. Once you're armed with the answers to these questions, you will be one step further towards choosing your colours.

- What is the function of the room? Are you going to work, live or sleep in it?
- How big or small is the room? For example, do you want to make it look larger or more intimate, higher or lower, longer or wider?
- What do you want these colours to do for you in this room? For example, do you need a cool, soothing colour or a stimulating, invigorating colour?
- And, last but not least: what do you like?

A little colour theory

Take a long look at the circle opposite. This colour wheel is based on three basic primary colours: red, blue and yellow. Together with black and white, these colours form the basic ingredients that create all colours. From pale tangerine to deep aubergine, the entire spectrum is mixed from the primaries, and black and white. This wheel is based on the discoveries of Johannes Itten, however, throughout history other theorists have organized colours in different ways. Sir Isaac Newton arranged them as a spectrum, Rudolph Steiner configured them in a circle, Goethe placed them in a triangle and Eastern theologies look at them in planes.

This one works quite simply. Complementary or opposite colours arise from mixing two primary colours, and placing them opposite the third. Red with yellow makes orange, which is the complementary colour to blue. Blue and yellow make green, the complementary colour to red. Red and blue make purple, which complements yellow. Complementary colours are directly opposite each other in the colour circle and make striking contrasts. Black makes a colour darker, while white makes it lighter. Adding more red or yellow to a colour makes it warmer, while adding more blue gives it a cooler quality. For definition's sake, a tint is a hue, such as blue, with white added, while a shade is a colour with black added. A tone is regarded as a colour with grey added. 'Chroma' is the intensity of a colour. Colour, as you see, has its own kind of language.

Additionally, there is further variation in:

- Tone (does a red tend towards orange or towards purple?)
- Saturation (how bright is it, how deep?)
- Brilliance (how dark or light is the colour, how much black or white does it contain?)

Illustration from: Johannes Itten – Kleurenleer ['Chromatics']

171

ALL ABOUT COLOUR

Remember the expression: red and green should never been seen? Well, think again. Colours never clash. Take Mother Nature, who often combines strange colours together that always coordinate naturally with each other. As we can see from the colour wheel, every colour affects another. A dark colour appears darker next to a light colour and a bright colour seems even brighter next to a complementary colour. Colours influence each other. The complementary combinations of red-green, yellow-purple and orange-blue constitute the brightest possible contrasts: they highlight each other.

The eye yearns for complementary colours: when you look at a red area and then close your eyes, your mind's eye shows you green. Colours can also exist in parallel to each other: pink or orange-red next to red, turquoise or blue-purple next to blue.

Graduations of one colour also look stunning. Colour combinations can be relaxed (and even relaxing) but can also add spice. Decide on exciting contrasts or more composed progressions in tone or choose subdued colours with, for example, sparkling highlights. To be able to experiment with colour you need to understand how colours react to one another.

Colours and their relationships

Combinations of colours differ greatly from one another, such as complementary colours. Very light and very dark colours, or cold and warm colours, bring depth to a dull room. Even in a monochrome (single colour) interior, you can add a powerful touch by simply picking out a small detail in a contrasting colour. As Mary Ward, creative director at international paint company Dulux says: 'If you want an energetic but stylish room, you can work with contrasting colours (opposite colours from the colour wheel). They are great for showcasing a feature or favourite piece of furniture. For example, a chocolate brown suede sofa contrasted with a teal blue looks stunning.'

Colour contrast Complementary colours have the most intense effect, as do colours widely separated from each other in the colour circle, such as blue with orange or blue with yellow. These combinations are powerful, stimulating and eye-catching. Green and purple are also very different but come much closer together the more they tend towards blue. And the closer these colours get to that blue, the subtler and yet more powerful they are.

If you are using extremely bright colours, it makes sense to balance them with large white or light-coloured surfaces, otherwise they become too overpowering and the effect is lost. For example, if you are painting one wall bright red and elsewhere you are working on orange or yellow accents, it might pay to have the other walls cream or a very soft yellow. Mary Ward sums it up: 'The trick with contemporary contrasting schemes is to balance the amount of each colour carefully, for example, using a larger quantity of a lighter colour balanced by a small injection of its contrasting colour in a deep shade is very powerful. Paint a focal wall in one strong shade and balance it with lighter shades of the contrasting colour.' Each colour needs to be balanced with neutrals or its opposite.

Cold-warm contrast Red, orange, yellow, pink and brown are warm colours. Green, blue-green, blue and purple are cool. By combining these hues, you can create beautiful contrasts.

Combinations of brown, red and orange (as in mahogany and earthenware) are usually associated with warmth and security. Many people feel comfortable amid less saturated shades of brown. Even the perceived temperature of a blue room against that of an orange room is different. In scientific tests it appeared that people thought it was a few degrees warmer in an orange room and a few degrees cooler in a blue room. Whether a colour appears warm or cold also depends on the colours surrounding it. Green is cold next to yellow but warm next to blue. Also, take into account the fact that warm colours, such as yellow and red, are more intense than a cool colour, such as blue. Consequently, a red-painted surface appears to leap out at you more than the same surface in blue, which is the very reason danger signals are a 'red alert'.

Light-dark contrast Place any colour next to a darker colour and it will immediately look lighter. By the same token, pastels appear stronger in colour when next to a white surface. In Rembrandt's paintings, deep colours glow because they have been set against yet darker colours. Light and dark are relative terms: they obtain that effect only when next to another contrasting colour or shade. Combining extremely light and dark colours can create a very unusual effect.

Shades, tints and tones

In addition to a combination of contrasting colours, you can also decorate a room in just one colour by merely using different shades or tones of the same colour. A monochromatic look uses the colour that sits right next to it on the colour wheel, and differs only slightly in lightness or darkness. The result is harmonious and calm, even with bright colours such as reds. Anyone wanting to experiment with a colourful interior would be wise to choose one colour in various shades of light and dark.

If you're worried this might be dull, don't be. Remember, colour is highlighted by the amount of light the room receives. A room in one colour tone projects an alternating interplay of colour when the light touches the surface. It's easy to prevent a single-toned effect from becoming listless. Just use a darker shade for the floor, a medium shade for the walls and a lighter shade for the ceiling. Or try experimenting with other contrasts besides this in terms of shapes, patterns, materials and textures. Monochrome colour combinations can also look fantastic in vibrant colours, particularly when contrasted with neutral shades like white or grey to provide an elegant touch.

Different tones The tonality of a colour depends upon the colours that have been mixed together to create it. For example, yellow can look green when it contains more blue, and orange when it contains more red. If you decide to use different tones of colour in combination, for example, pure blue with greenish blue and purplish blue, the effect is luxurious.

Different shades A room can be made more restful using one main colour in different gradations of intensity. The whiter the room, the more restful it is. Picture these combinations together: red, dark red and pink, or blue, dark blue and light blue.

COLOUR AND LIGHT

The mood of a room can alter with the changing light. Things you should look out for include:

Time of day Think about the time of day when the room is going to be used most, and make your choice of colours according to that type of light. Check early in the morning, then around midday and again in the evening, to see how much light your room receives and from which angle it comes. The warmth of colour changes from hour to hour. Early in the morning, the emphasis is on shades of blue. Throughout the course of the day this tends more to white and yellow, and by the evening to red. Furthermore, colours appear more yellow by electric light than by daylight. This is why we often take a moment to hold clothing up to the daylight in a shop window before making a purchase.

Quantity of light Look at the number of windows and how much light touches different surfaces. In a room with few windows you are better off choosing a colour that looks good in electric light. If the light from outside is too bright, filter it by using blinds or an awning.

North-facing rooms The light entering a north-facing room is cool, so warm colours work best here.

South- and west-facing rooms A white room facing south reflects the light intensely, which can make the use of brilliant white too harsh. Sunlight sometimes over emphasizes bright colours. As a result, pastels are sometimes bright enough for south-facing rooms – as are cool colours.

Latitude White and grey look cooler in more northerly regions.

Type of electric light If you are taking electric light into consideration, think about the type of bulb you will be using. As a rule, halogen bulbs are the most similar to daylight. Energy-saving bulbs often have a yellowish glow, while fluorescent strip lighting can be bluish and rather cold. Nowadays, there are different bulbs for different looks from cool to warm.

COLOUR AND SPACE

Experiencing any space is unconsciously influenced by colour. Warm colours have the illusion of advancing spaces, while cooler colours recede. You can manipulate a room's length, breadth and height simply by using different colours.

Large or small A black car appears smaller than a white one. In the same way, a dark room appears smaller than a light one. Light floors and ceilings make a room appear larger because they reflect light. A light ceiling with a dark floor creates a more solid base for furniture.

175

Light or dark A dark room appears lighter if its walls and ceiling are light in colour. A black ceiling has a lowering effect. In contrast, a white ceiling reflects ten to fifteen per cent more light than a ceiling painted in a colour. It also makes the ceiling seem higher, creating a feeling of spaciousness.

Spacious colours The vaulting in European gothic cathedrals was often painted light blue. This was done to suggest heaven above, but it also created a greater spatial effect because of blue's 'recessive' properties. A warm red surface appears to advance towards you, while a blue surface recedes. Warm colours advance, making a room more intimate; cool colours have the opposite effect, making a room appear more spacious. Red, red-violet, orange-red, orange, orange-yellow and yellow make rooms smaller and cosier. So use cool colours if the room needs to look bigger: violet, blue-green, blue, green, or colours containing a lot of white. A home also appears roomier if you use the same colour throughout. If you feel this might be a little monochrome, try painting all the woodwork the same colour instead, as this, too, gives a feeling of unity.

Paint effects You can make a ceiling appear lower when you don't paint the topmost 25cm (10in) from the top of the walls. Or, you can elevate the roof with vertical stripes. Horizontal stripes on a short stretch of wall widen the room. You can also emphasize particular functional areas within a room by demarcating sections of floor and walls with different shades. When you paint a dining area's floor in red and the living room in blue, for example, the eye creates a visual divide.

COLOUR AND FORM

Colour can do so much more to transform a room that just paint its walls and floors. These spaces are by far the largest canvases in a room but cleverly painted accessories and flashes of colour in surprising places create illusion and drama. Sometimes, using bright colours as a graphic detail are much more dramatic than just slapping brightly coloured paint on a wall. Black can suddenly come

Aubergine

to life on a distinctively designed piece of furniture. White cupboards are transformed when contrasted with a bright colour on the inside. Painting a wall with abstract shapes or a line from your favourite poem gives a room a lift. The possibilities are endless. You get fast results for little cost and the best thing is that if you're not happy, just paint over it. It's all a question of trial and error.

Squares With the help of masking tape, it's easy to paint squares or other angular shapes straight on to a wall. With the help of a friend, just place a piece of tape on the wall. Each of you needs to take one end, pull the tape taut and press down on each end. Lightly press down on the tape with your fingertips. You can check whether the shapes are straight using a spirit level. Afterwards, all you have to do is paint in the shapes and carefully remove the masking tape.

Stripes A band of harmonious and contrasting colours in the form of horizontal stripes creates a dynamic, cheerful room. Prevent an overdose of colour by restricting stripes to one wall. Paint stripes neatly with the help of masking tape or go freehand to emphasize their informality.

Circles Make circles easily by making a home-made compass. Tie a piece of string to a pencil and stick a pin through the string at the length that will be the radius of the circle (half the full length diameter). Stick the pin in the wall and use the pencil to draw the circle. Alternatively, do the same on a piece of card, cut out the circle and use the card as a stencil.

Other patterns and drawings Sketch these freehand on the wall or, to make it easier, use an overhead projector. Draw your subject on a transparent sheet of plastic and project it on to the wall. Transfer the drawing to the wall using a hard pencil. If you make a mistake, you can remove it with a damp cloth and some detergent (pencil erasers leave an oily mark). If you do not have an overhead projector, use a slide projector. Photograph your subject on a slide and project it on to the wall.

Dado effect Create a different spatial effect by painting the wall horizontally in two complementary colours (a dado). Wainscoting or a raised skirting board is rendered easily in paint with the help of masking tape to create a straight line. Stretch the tape, as described above under 'Squares', and check the line with a spirit level.

Shapes on canvas If you're not keen to paint directly onto the wall, or suspect you may want to move the shapes around, try painting a piece of artist's canvas – wall paints are perfect for this. The simplest way is to paint the canvas in one colour: for example, you could put up a large grey rectangle on a white wall or a series of squares, one next to the other in different colours. For more texture, you could cut out shapes in plywood, paint them in bright colours and hang them next to each other. For textured effects, add a collage of wrapping papers, wools, sequins or ribbons.

Experimenting with gloss Paint a design on top of a colourful wall, but instead of using another colour try the sheen of a colourless, transparent gloss. A square, circle, or broad stripe, for example in a mother-of-pearl gloss paint, will look beautiful. The effect is very subtle and looks fantastic when the light hits the wall, plus with extra light reflecting around the room, it will look even bigger.

Text Write a line from your favourite play or poem on the wall, or even just your favourite word. Begin by making sure the text will be even by drawing a horizontal line on the wall in pencil. Experiment on paper before writing out your text in pencil freehand to see if it works or not. A projector can come in handy.

Paper effect To create a paper effect, paint the wall in an extremely pale colour. Then, using wallpaper paste, apply thin sheets of slightly crinkled tissue paper of the same colour. Try this on just one section of a wall at a time – this works better in small doses.

PAINT

In addition to 'ordinary' paint, there is paint for the senses. Textured paint is not only looks good, but feels good too. Create a sensuous experience for both the eye and fingertips.

Sand-textured paint A fine dusting of sand on your walls not only provides unusual texture but also plays tricks with the light. Buy these ready-made as a matt-velvet textured paint where the sand only shows up on the second coat. Apply the first coat with a paint roller or pad and let it dry evenly, then only use a paint pad for the second coat. Try stripes in different directions for a random texture, or repeated semicircular arcs for more regularity.

Stucco-textured paint Bring the outside in with a stucco effect. Available in various shades of white, this rolls on smoothly with a matt finish.

Gloss and glitter For an extravagant opulence, try gold or silver paint. It gives a wonderful sheen to walls and ceilings. Covering the walls in just one coat, it is easiest to apply with a wide roller. You could also try glitter paint iin small areas or a transparent mother-of-pearl paint that changes in the light and gives walls and ceilings a wonderful, vibrant sheen. This paint is applied over another colour using a short-pile emulsion (smooth latex) roller. The result is pure luxury.

Choosing paint

The green of linden trees in the spring, the red of your first party dress, the blue of your grandmother's wallpaper: we all relate to colour on an emotional level. And we all have our own private colour spectrum. But the trick for brilliant interiors is to translate these colours into paint. You have to be able to refer to colours in a specific language that both you and the paint manufacturer understand. That's why some brands use the ACC Code, which precisely identifies a colour within the spectrum. This is not only useful for recognizing a particular colour, but also if a particular paint is withdrawn from the market it should still be possible to mix it based upon this code.

In order to choose colours successfully you need to have an understanding of your style and feel confident enough to use it. To help decide what colours you like, look at the following tips:

● Be inspired by your favourite painting or piece of furniture.

● Take note of the unconscious colour choices you have already made in your life. The colour of your car, the clothes you wear, your favourite fruit. Collect postcards, pictures from magazines – any images and colours you like the look of. Stick your favourites into a scrapbook.

● Always check the paint samples in the room where you want to use the colour. Never make a definitive choice in the store since the light will be totally different.

● If you use the room mainly in the evening, check the colour under an electric light.

● Always buy test pots wherever possible. Painting approximately one square metre (three square feet) should give you a good idea of a colour's end result.

● Paint radiators or other unattractive objects in the room the same colour as the wall to make them less obtrusive. These objects will then quietly blend in.

● Always buy sufficient quantities of paint for the area you are decorating in one go, as different batches of the same paint can vary slightly. Make sure you always have some paint left over to repair any damages caused in the future.

- Painting walls, floors, and ceiling all the same colour, intensifies that colour by at least fifty per cent. So, consider using a slightly less saturated version than shown on the guide.
- Use a lot of white to balance a colour scheme. If you like strong, bright colours, keep floors and ceilings neutral to prevent the walls and windows creating colour discordance.
- If you are worried about using too much colour, just start small. Try accenting neutral shades with a bright cushion, or a throw. Perhaps touch up a section of a wall or one small surface with colour. And remember, paint is soon painted over again if it's not what you wanted.
- Don't restrict yourself to paint in gloss and matt forms. Many paint brands offer traditional paints, like Chinese lacquer paints, distemper (the forerunner of emulsion) and limewashes. There's also craquelure, which gives the impression of cracked paintwork, once popular in the eighteenth century. Modern paint finishes include cord, suede or denim, all of which look very hip on contemporary walls.

Preparation and materials

A good paint job is all in the preparation, so read this section with care. Often this takes as long as painting, but unless you pay attention to every detail, the flaws will undermine the look, quality and longevity of your paint job. A smooth surface will give you a smooth finish.

Prepare the surface A coat of paint won't correct an unloved surface. The surface must be scrubbed thoroughly before any painting. You can buy special cleaners to remove dirt, grease or nicotine stains.

Blistering Clean up past mistakes. In rooms where the old wall paint has blistered, emulsion (latex) paint will probably have been used without a primer. This means sanding back the blisters and then preparing the wall using a special primer before applying any wall paint.

Over-absorbent surfaces Always test whether your wall is likely to absorb a lot of paint by spraying water onto the surface with a plant sprayer. If the water is absorbed into the wall quickly this means it will probably also absorb an excessive amount of paint. Always apply a primer coat first.

Damp patches Have the damp checked by a professional before you start. Ordinary wall paint will never cover damp patches and water marks and when water comes through it will ruin your work.

Glazed wall tiles These should be scoured, cleaned and pre-treated with a special tile primer.

Damaged wood surface, wood with nail holes Cover in primer, sand well and apply varnish filler with a filling knife. Afterwards, prime once again, then paint over.

Concrete floors Bring the floor back to the plain concrete surface by removing all the dust and dirt with a sander. Then use a paint designed for use on concrete.

Bare wood Sand rough surfaces with a medium-grade sandpaper and wipe away any dust with a damp cloth. Next, apply a coat of water to the wood with a wet cloth. Allow it to dry, then sand with fine paper to remove any raised grain. Apply a stain-blocking primer and let it dry before you begin.

Wallpapered surfaces Remove the wallpaper by peeling, soaking, scraping or steaming it off. Scrub off any glue and rinse thoroughly. You may need to sand down any gullies or blisters. You'll need to apply an interior or solvent-based or water-based stain-blocking sealer before painting.

Metal surfaces, radiators, pipes Scour and sand down till smooth. Paint with a special metal paint.

Rusty metal surfaces Remove the rust, then scour thoroughly and sand down. Brush on a metal primer, then use a paint recommended for metal.

Dealing with lead-based paint Although uncommon these days, do keep in mind that lead-based paints were commonly used in houses until the mid-Fifties and, as if that wasn't enough, red lead was used in primers until the Eighties. If you are removing lead paint, you must use dust sheets to catch all the debris and regularly clean up as you go. This is toxic work, so wear goggles and a surgical mask. Seek expert advice from your local DIY store before you start.

Hard plastic Scour, sand down and apply plastic primer. Then just paint over.

Plastic kitchen cabinets Scour and lightly sand down. Afterwards, apply primer that is specially designed for use on plastic. Any paint can then be applied, and with fantastic effects.

Brushes and rollers Even when you buy the very best wall paint, the result is disappointing if you use the wrong brush or roller. Use a paint pad or roller to apply wall paint. Lambswool emulsion (latex) rollers are suitable for smooth, rough or textured surfaces. Woodwork is best painted using a brush, then after an even coating, you can go over it again with a roller. Use a lambswool pile (nap) roller to apply emulsion (latex) paint and a smooth foam roller to apply gloss paint. As ever, when it comes to buying the right roller or paint brush, quality costs, but it's worth it.

Preparing previously painted surfaces Inspect closely, watching out for flaking, cracking, peeling, or chipped paint. You may need to remove the paint with a scraper, a tried and tested method for flat surfaces, or a stiff wire brush. With either method you'll need to use a fine sandpaper afterwards.

Old, flaking coats of paint on woodwork Use paint stripper and before sanding wash down well with a special wood rinse. Afterwards, prime and then paint.

After painting Firmly seal the can of paint after use. Store it upside down, as this will prevent a skin from forming on the surface. If you plan to continue painting the next day, wrap your brush in kitchen foil or seal your roller in a plastic bag. The following day you will be able to carry on painting as before. Once finished, you can clean a brush used for an oil-based paint with turpentine. If you have used wall paint or acrylic paint, clean the brush or roller in a bucket of water, let the paint sink to the bottom and dispose of it as chemical waste in an appropriate rubbish tip.